2017
Merry Christmas
Joanna,
Lots of Love
& Happiness in the New
Year!
Love,
Stevie

DAILY STRENGTHS FOR DAILY NEEDS

First published by Parragon in 2010

Parragon
Queen Street House
4 Queen Street
Bath BA1 1HE, UK

Copyright © Parragon Books Ltd 2009
Design by Pink Creative Ltd

ISBN: 978-1-4075-8640-3

Printed in China

DAILY STRENGTHS
FOR DAILY NEEDS

A COLLECTION OF MOTIVATIONAL
QUOTES AND IMAGES

Bath · New York · Singapore · Hong Kong · Cologne · Delhi · Melbourne

Early to bed and early to rise makes a man healthy, wealthy, and wise.

Benjamin Franklin,
One of the Founding Fathers of the United
States of America.

Make the most of yourself, for that is all there is of you.

Ralph Waldo Emerson,
Essayist, philosopher and poet

A gentle breeze

blowing in the right direction

is better than a pair

of strong oars.

Canary Island proverb

If you do not hope,
you will not find
what is beyond
your hopes.

St. Clement of Alexandria

A strong person and a waterfall always channel their own path.

Unknown

We are still **masters** of our fate.

We are still **captains** of our souls.

Winston Churchill, Former Prime Minister

Happiness is when what you think, what you say, and what you do are in harmony.

Mahatma Gandhi, political and spiritual leader of India

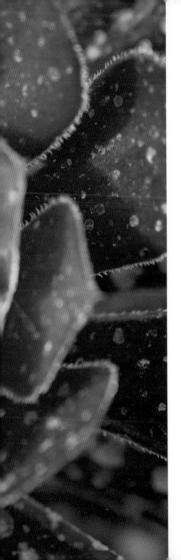

Be not afraid
of growing slowly,
be afraid only
of standing still.

Chinese proverb

Your vision will become **clear**
only when you look into your heart.

Who looks outside, dreams.
Who looks inside, awakens.

Carl Gustav Jung, Psychiatrist

Life is not measured
by the breaths we take,
but by the moments
that take our breath.

Unknown

23

The best and most
beautiful things
in the world cannot be seen
or even touched.

They must be felt with the heart.

Hellen Keller, Author, political activist and lecturer

Don't judge

those who try and fail,

judge those

who fail to try.

Unknown

Never look down on anyone unless you're helping him up.

Jesse Jackson,
American Civil rights activist
and Baptist minister

No act of **kindness**,

however small,

is ever wasted.

Unknown

A pessimist

sees the difficulty in every opportunity;

an optimist

sees the opportunity in every difficulty.

Unknown

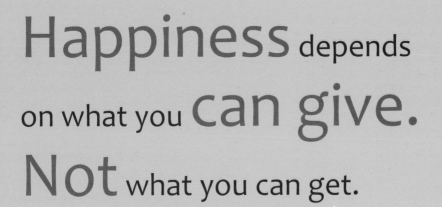

Happiness depends on what you can give. Not what you can get.

Mahatma Gandhi, political and spiritual leader of India

Think of all
the beauty
still left
around you
and be happy.

Anne Frank,
Diarist and fugitive of the Third Reich

The more light
you allow within you,

the brighter the world
you live in will be.

Shakti Gawain, Author

Never live
in the past

but always
learn from it.

Unknown

Take heed:
you do not find
what you do not seek.

Proverb

Pull the string,

and it will follow

wherever you wish.
Push it, and it will go
nowhere at all.

Dwight D. Eisenhower, Former President
of the United States of America

He who lives
in harmony with himself
lives in harmony
with the world.

Marcus Aurelius, Roman Emperor

Things today

may not be great,

but they are not bad,

and that's good.

There are only two ways
to live your life.
One is as though
nothing is a miracle.
The other is as though
everything is a miracle.

Albert Einstein, Physicist

A life spent making mistakes is not only

more honourable,

but more useful

than a life spent doing nothing.

George Bernard Shaw, Playwright

We make
a living
by what
we get,
we make
a life
by what
we give.

Winston Churchill, Former Prime Minister

Let us be grateful to people who make us happy; they are the charming gardeners who make our souls blossom.

Marcel Proust, Novelist

Courage doesn't always roar.
Sometimes courage is
the quiet voice
at the end of the day saying,
"I will try again tomorrow."

Mary Anne Radmacher

Failure is taking the path that everyone else does, **success** is making your **own path.**

Unknown

Life isn't about $finding$ yourself.

Life is about creating yourself.

George Bernard Shaw, Playright

Imagination will often carry us to worlds that never were. But without it we go nowhere.

Carl Sagan, Astronomer

Experience is the child of thought, and thought is the child of action.

Benjamin Disraeli, Former Prime Minister

What you see depends on
what you're looking for.

Unknown

Teach us delight
 in simple things,
and mirth that has
 no bitter springs.

Rudyard Kipling, Author and poet

What lies behind us
and what lies before us
are tiny matters compared
to what lies within us.

Walt Emerson, Artist and educator

There is no greatness
where there is not simplicity.

Leo Tolstoy, Novelist

With the new day comes

new strengths and new thoughts

Eleanor Roosevelt, Former First Lady of the United States of America

Peace comes from within.
Do not seek it without it.

Gautama Siddharta, Buddha Spiritual leader

Be faithful in small things
because it is in them
that your strength lies.

Mother Teresa, Roman Catholic Nun and humanitarian

Anyone who has never made a mistake has never tried anything new.

Albert Einstein, Physicist

Anyone can hold the helm

when the sea is calm.

Unknown

He who hesitates

is lost.

Proverb

In seed time learn,

in harvest teach,

in winter enjoy.

William Blake, Poet

Confidence comes not from

always being right,

but from not fearing

to be wrong.

Unknown

Everything you do
can be done better
from a place of relaxation.

Stephen C Paul, Writer

Have regular hours for work and play;
make each day both useful and pleasant,
and prove that you understand the worth
if time by employing it well.

Then youth will be delightful,
old age will bring few regrets and life
will become a beautiful success,
in spite of poverty.

Louise May Alcott, Author of *Little Women*

Picture credits

My Actions Matter

A Book on Life Values

Other Books in the Can-Do Kid Series

My Body's Mine

I Can Do That!

Other Books By Kayla J.W. Marnach

Learning Lyrics,
Workbook and CD

Come to the Gathering
Anthology

My First Aid Book

**For more information,
please contact:**
http://www.kaylajwmarnach.com

My Actions Matter

A book on Life Values

Kayla J.W. Marnach

With a foreword by: Brandi Winters, LCSW

Illustrated by Kate Collazo

YANA Press

My Actions Matter
A Book on Life Values

Derived from:
TBRI-Trust Based Relational Intervention ®
TCU Institute of Child Development
Texas Christian University
TCCC-Travis County
Collaborative for Children

Printed in the United States of America

YANA Press, Austin, Texas

Dedication

Having the knowledge of how to appropriately interact with others is not a skill we are born with. Those skills must be learned. And to teach our children effectively we need to provide them scripts they can use to discern what behavior is best for them and others around them.

This book is dedicated to caregivers who want to empower their child with the social skills necessary to create enduring connections, and experience a life lived with respect and trust.

Foreword

My Actions Matter teaches children a foundation of life values, and these can shape behaviors when difficult situations arise. By learning these life values, children are empowered to connect with others in a safe and respectful manner. The strategies presented in *My Actions Matter* will have lasting impacts on the child's life.

As a licensed clinical social worker, I use *My Actions Matter* as part of my professional counseling practice with children and their families. I encourage caregivers to read and practice the strategies for keeping values present in everyday interactions with others. Children love the sing-song rhythm and diverse characters created in the book, and adults appreciate this fun and easy tool for practicing life values.

Included in the back of the book is a Behaviors Display A Need section which brings a deeper understanding about creating life values. The Questions and Explorations section suggests easy to implement activities for caregivers to use with their children. They are simple but powerful.

This is a wonderful book that creates a foundation of kindness and respect in a fun, relatable format. I thoroughly delight in reading *My Actions Matter* in session as well as with my own children.

Brandi Winters, LCSW

My Actions
Matter

It's good to know just what to do,
To have a plan for **me.**

It makes me **stop** and want to try
To do what's **best** for me.

I use my **words** and show respect.
I'm gentle and **kind,**
it's **true.**

I cooperate

and **compromise.**

I **know** that you can, **too!**

ccepting no and who's the **boss,**

I listen and **obey.**

It's good to know
we cause no hurts.

Life's **happier**
this way.

And when I don't act like I should,
But then correct my ways,

It's **good** to know
we let it **go**

And **lift** our hands
in praise!

3

Sometimes it's hard to share my toys.
I want them all for me.
I yell or scream or throw a fit!
I'm unhappy as can be.

But, then comes in a safe adult,
To show a better way.
They help me stop and do what's right,
And this is what they say,

"Please, use your words and show respect. Please, listen and obey.

We'll talk about a compromise,

But I'm the boss, today."

5

It's good to know just what to do,
To have a plan for me.

It makes me stop and want to try
To do what's best for me.

I use my words and show respect.
I'm gentle and kind, it's true.

I cooperate
and compromise.
I know that you can, too!

ccepting no and who's the boss,

I listen and obey.

It's good to know
we cause no hurts.

Life's happier
this way.

And when I don't act like I should,

But then correct my ways,

It's good to know

we let it go

And lift our hands

in praise!

7

Sometimes I'm rough
with kids or things,
And even pets, it's true.
I squeeze too hard,
or push or pull,
Do what I
shouldn't do.

But, then comes in a safe adult,
Who helps me stop to see
That I might hurt or harm someone
So, then they say to me,

"We cause no hurts.
We use our words.
Cooperate this way.
Be gentle and kind
with everything.

We act
no other way."

It's good to know just what to do,
To have a plan for me.

It makes me stop and want to try
To do what's best for me.

I use my words
and show respect.
I'm gentle and kind,
it's true.

I cooperate

and compromise.

I know that you can, too!

Accepting no and who's the boss,
I listen and obey.

It's good to know
we cause no hurts.
Life's happier
this way.

And when I don't act like I should,
But then correct my ways,

It's good to know
we let it go

And lift our hands
in praise!

I can be sassy with my words,
With looks and **attitude.**

With hands on hips,

I roll my eyes.

My words are **really** rude.

And then there is my safe adult,

"Oh whoa!"

they say,

"No way!"

"Let's try again now,
with respect."
I listen and obey.

So, then I change my attitude.
I know just what to do.
"I'm sorry that my tone was mean.
I'd like a quick redo."

It's good to know just what to do,
To have a plan for me.

It makes me stop and want to try
To do what's best for me.

I use my words
and show respect.
I'm gentle and kind,
it's true.

I cooperate
and compromise.
I know that you can, too!

Accepting no and who's the boss,
I listen and obey.

It's good to know
we cause no hurts.

Life's happier
this way.

And when I don't act like I should,
But then correct my ways,

It's good to know
we let it go

And lift our hands
in praise!

BEHAVIORS DISPLAY A NEED

Lead by example. Display the desired behavior you want from your child to provide a model for them to follow.

These life values are not inherent but learned. Acquiring and instilling these desired behaviors require reliable reinforcement. Consistent application creates an environment of security and trust. These skills impact every area of life and are invaluable in our child's ability to connect with others. By teaching your child life values, you provide them the tools to connect meaningfully to others, impacting their world today and in the future. **KEY POINT:** Your child is NOT their behavior. Their behavior displays a need and as the caregiver it is up to you to discover and meet that need. When needs are met, appropriate behaviors are displayed.

1. DO NOT OVER REACT. When your child is acting disrespectful, respectfully engage them. Speaking in a playful tone keeps the behavior from escalating. By stating, "Oh, my, let's try that again with a respectful tone or respectful face," or another engaging statement, you acknowledge the behavior is not accepted. Follow the statement by providing an opportunity for them to correct that behavior. By you not over reacting, your child is more open to listening. **KEY POINT:** Engage with your child in a calm and respectful manner. The goal is to model the behavior you want to see in your child. Remember, children learn to mirror our modeling.

2. FOCUSED ENGAGEMENT. Maintaining control of your behavior is key when you are met with resistance from your child, because you are modeling how to handle difficult situations. Move down to your child's eye level. If your child refuses to look at you, gently touch their cheek or chin, encouraging them to look into your eyes. With a calm but firm voice, provide a choice or compromise allowing your child to have a voice in resolving the issue using a statement such as, "You need to pick up your toys, so do you want to start with the ones over here or over there?" or "It's time for bed, so which book do you want to read?" **KEY POINT:** Choices and compromises empower the child, thereby providing buy-in from them, creating a win-win situation.

3. CALM IT DOWN. When a child loses their control, becomes dysregulated, it is vital you remain calm with complete focus on the child. With a firm tone and in as few words as possible make your wishes known. Acknowledge you understand they are upset and tell them you are going to help them by giving them a place to think about their behavior. Keep them nearby in a safe place so they will not feel abandoned. Once you witness they are calm, go back to focused engagement. **KEY POINT:** Follow through is vital. The situation is resolved when your child understands the desired behavior and can reengage calmly and safely.

4. PROTECT FROM HARM. When the child or another in the vicinity might be harmed by your child's behavior, you must remain calm and take immediate action. Remove your child from the area and remain with them until they return to a calm state. Encourage the child to breathe, confirming you know they are upset and you want to understand what it is they need. Everyone has an agenda and when an adult without warning demands compliance without respecting the child, unwanted behaviors can occur. Therefore, treat your child as you want to be treated. **KEY POINT:** Protecting children from harm is our number one priority. But in the process, we must be sure we are not harming the child whose behavior is in question.

5. WHEN IT'S OVER...IT'S OVER. Once the situation is resolved and the behavior displayed has been addressed, do NOT bring it up again – E.V.E.R.!!! By "Lifting our hands in praise," you acknowledge the goal has been met and the situation has been resolved. The only way it should be brought up again is acknowledging their success, never their failure. **KEY POINT:** The past is the past and that's where it belongs.

QUESTIONS AND EXPLORATIONS

Ask your child the following open-ended questions. Make sure to listen and repeat back what they say to confirm you understand their answer.

1. USE MY WORDS

    a. Why do you think it's important to use your words instead of whining?

    b. What tone of voice is best when using your words?

2. SHOW RESPECT

    a. What does it mean to be respectful of others? To be disrespectful?

    b. How do you show proper respect?

3. BE GENTLE

    a. Why is it important to be gentle?

    b. Can you show me a gentle action?

4. BE KIND

    a. Why should we be kind to one another?

    b. How do you feel when others are kind to you? When you're treated unkindly?

5. COOPERATE

    a. Why should you cooperate with others?

    b. How does it make you feel when others cooperate with you?

6. COMPROMISE

    a. What is a compromise?

    b. Why is it important to learn to compromise?

    c. What do you do when you are asked to compromise?

7. ACCEPTING NO

    a. Why is it important to accept no from a safe adult?

    b. What can you do if you are upset about a safe adult telling you no?

8. WHO'S THE BOSS

    a. What safe adults do you know that can boss you?

    b. Why is it important to accept that they can boss you?

9. LISTEN

    a. Why do you like others to listen to you?

    b. Why is it important to listen to safe adults?

10. OBEY

    a. Why should you obey safe adults?

    b. How do you act when you don't want to obey a safe adult?

11. CAUSE NO HURTS

    a. Why is it important to not hurt others with our words? Our body?

    b. What do you do if someone hurts you?

12. LET IT GO

    a. What is the best part about not being reminded about your past behaviors?

ACTIVITES: *Role play is one of the most engaging and memorable activities you can do with your child. Take turns role playing the above questions, switching off acting out the negative and the positive of each behavior. Make it a fun activity and let their imagination take the lead.*

ABOUT THE AUTHOR

A native Texan, Kayla lives with her husband and three cats in Austin, Texas. Her husband and two married daughters, along with her faith, have been an inspiration in many of her writings. She has been a guest speaker at elementary schools, women's retreats, writer's groups, and the University of Texas. At the request of teachers and counselors, she has provided stories broaching difficult situations. Her passion is to empower and validate children, helping them know they are not alone in their feelings or circumstances. Her goal is to share ways children can make positive decisions about their actions and understand and work with their feelings.

When she is not writing she loves spending time with family and friends, reading, scrapbooking, and watching old movies.

ABOUT THE ILLUSTRATOR

Graphic Designer and Digital Illustrator, Kate Collazo, lives in Austin Texas with her husband and two Dachshunds. She enjoys paddle boarding, motorcycling, and all kinds of other outdoor activities. Kate loves being close to family and is inspired to do work for the Can-Do Kids Series by her beloved nieces and nephews whom she adores.

34690048R00020

Made in the USA
Middletown, DE
28 January 2019